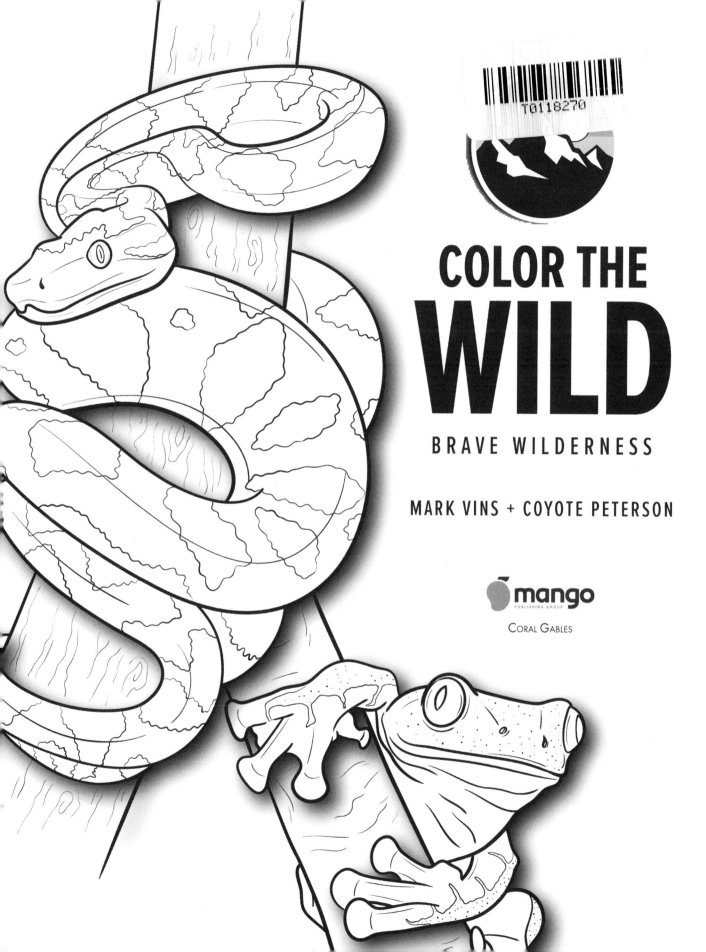

COLOR THE
WILD

BRAVE WILDERNESS

MARK VINS + COYOTE PETERSON

mango
PUBLISHING GROUP

CORAL GABLES

For permission requests, please contact the publisher at:
Mango Publishing Group
2850 S Douglas Road, 4th Floor
Coral Gables, FL 33134 USA
info@mango.bz

For special orders, quantity sales, course adoptions and corporate sales, please email the publisher at sales@mango.bz. For trade and wholesale sales, please contact Ingram Publisher Services at customer.service@ingramcontent.com or +1.800.509.4887.

Color the Wild: Brave Wilderness Coloring Pages

ISBN: (print) 978-1-68481-017-8
BISAC category code: JNF001010, JUVENILE NONFICTION / Activity Books / Coloring

THIS BOOK BELONGS TO:

_____

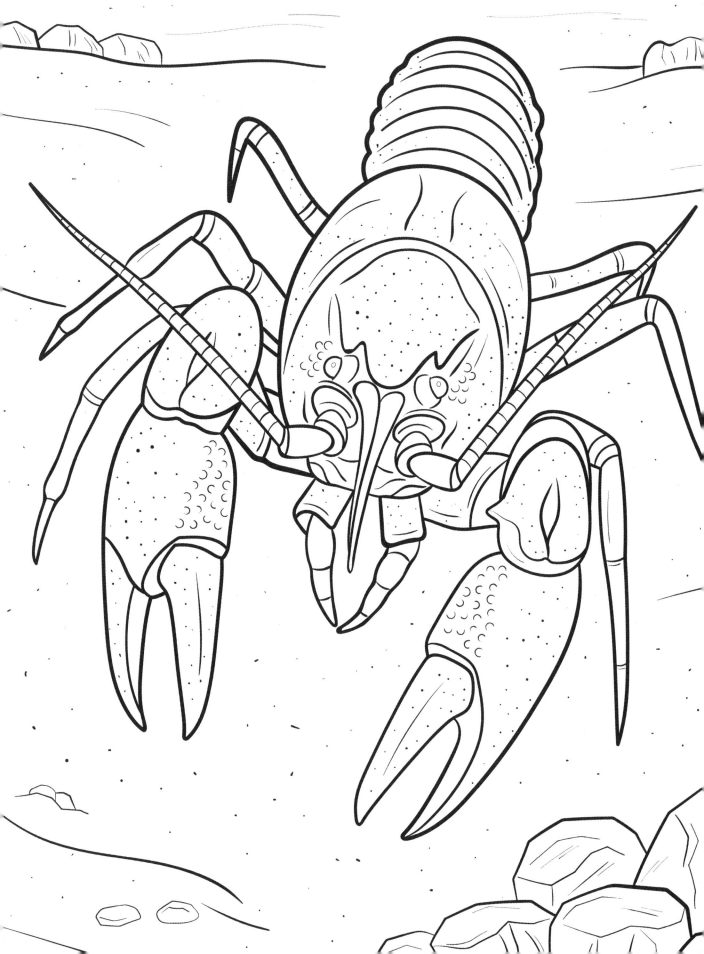

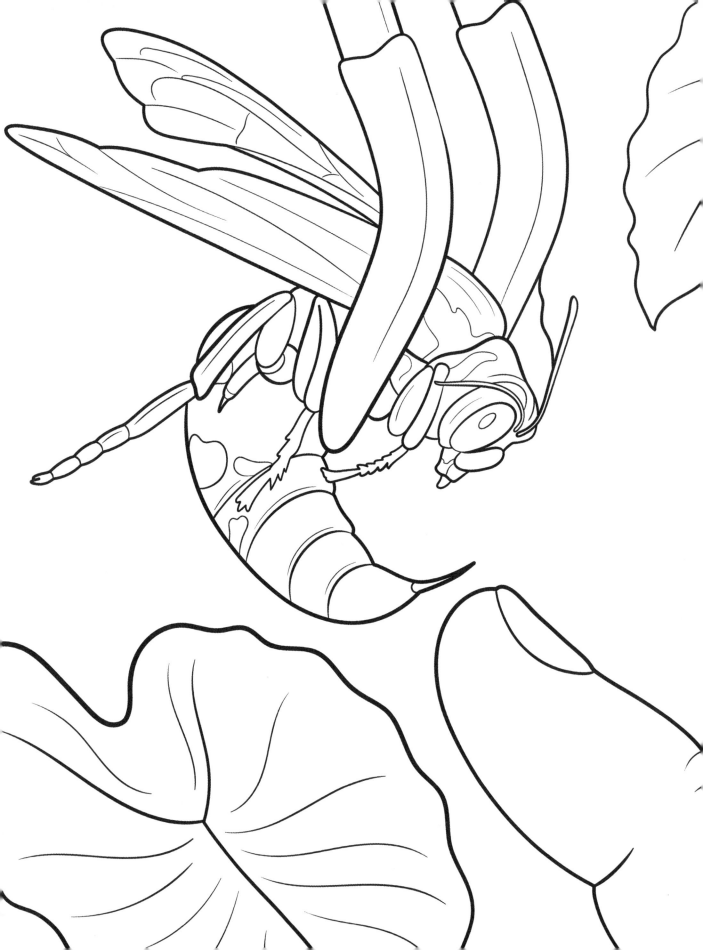

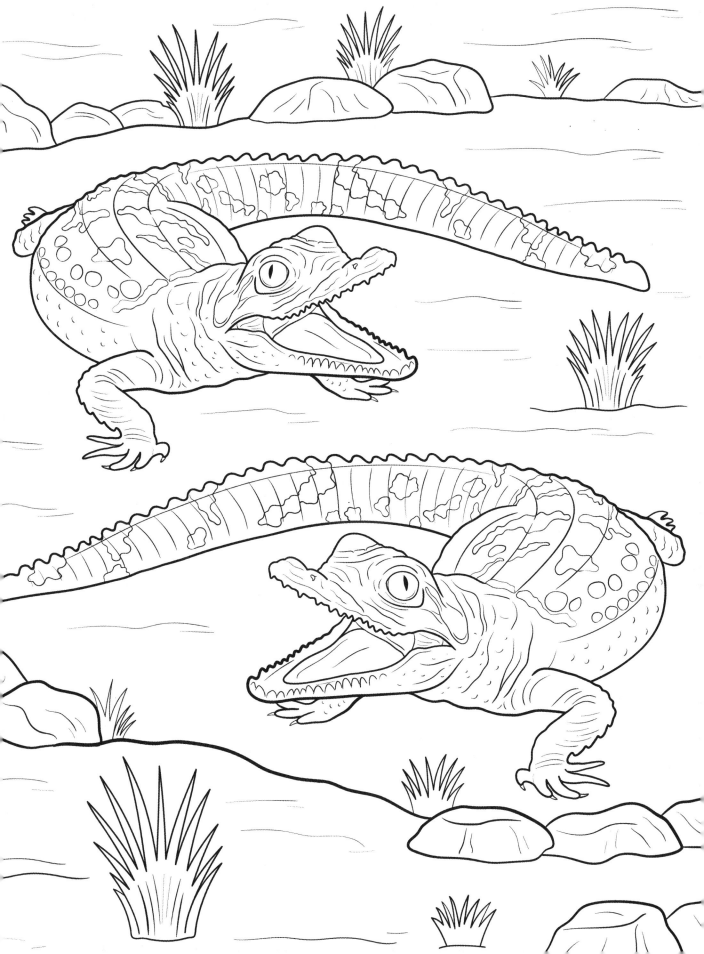

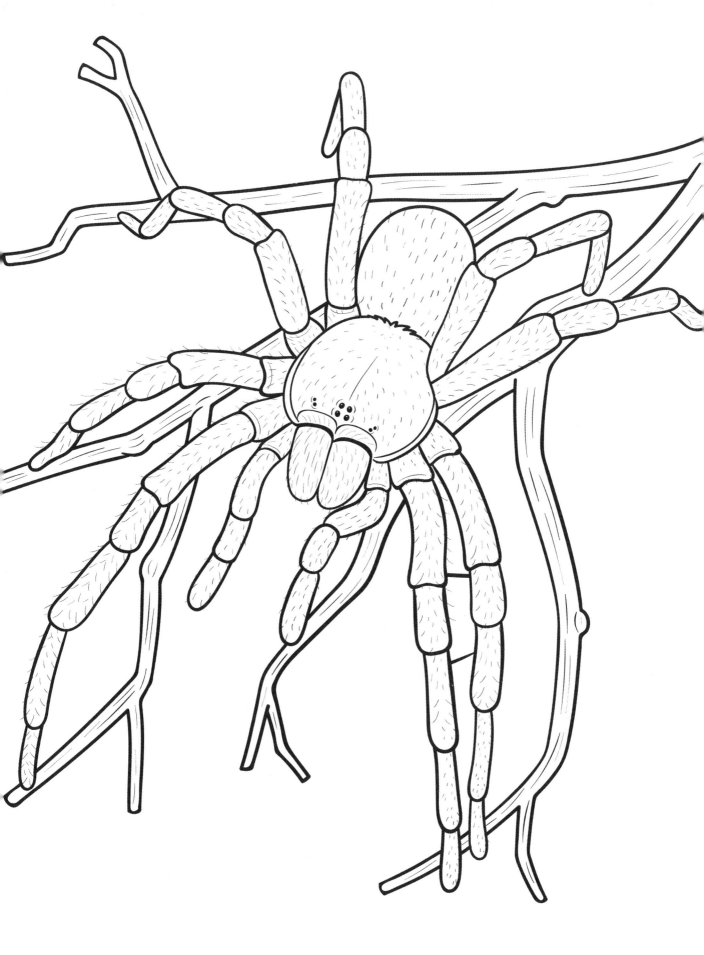

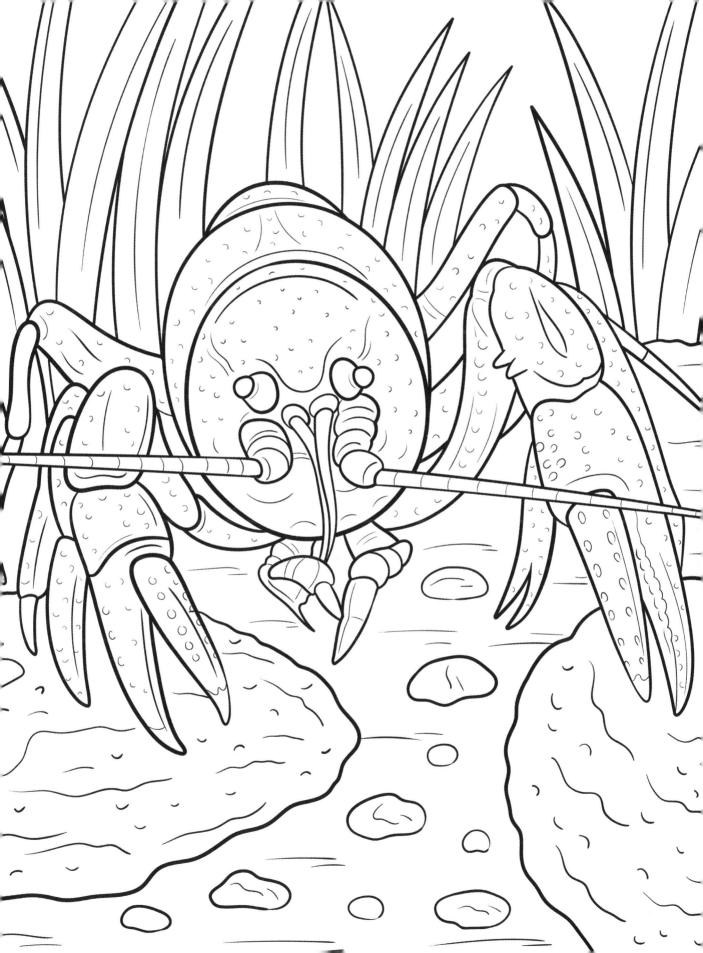

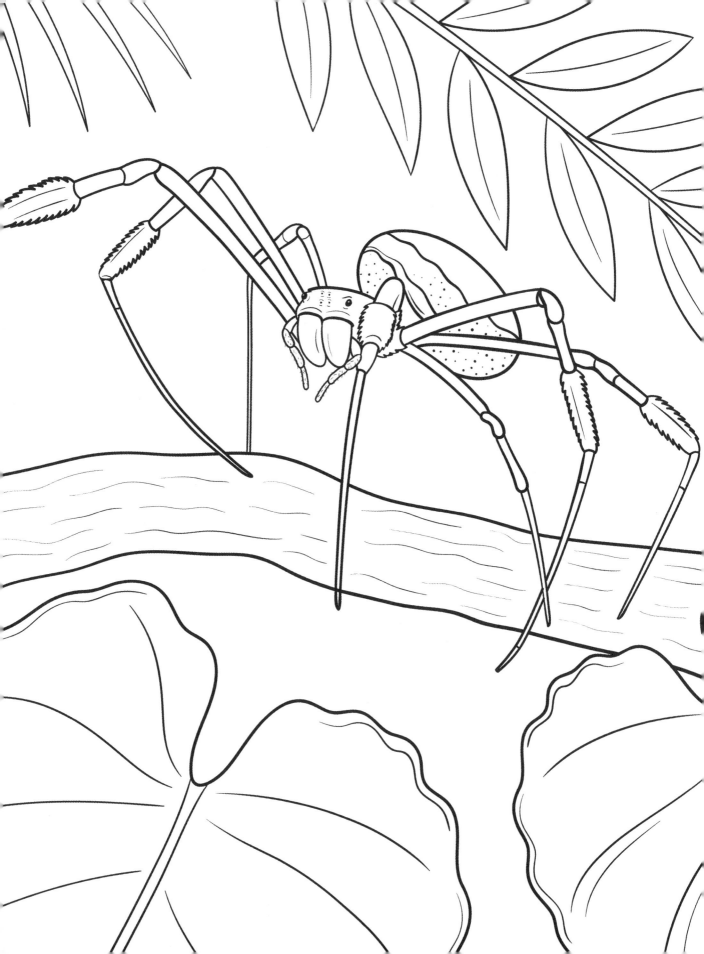

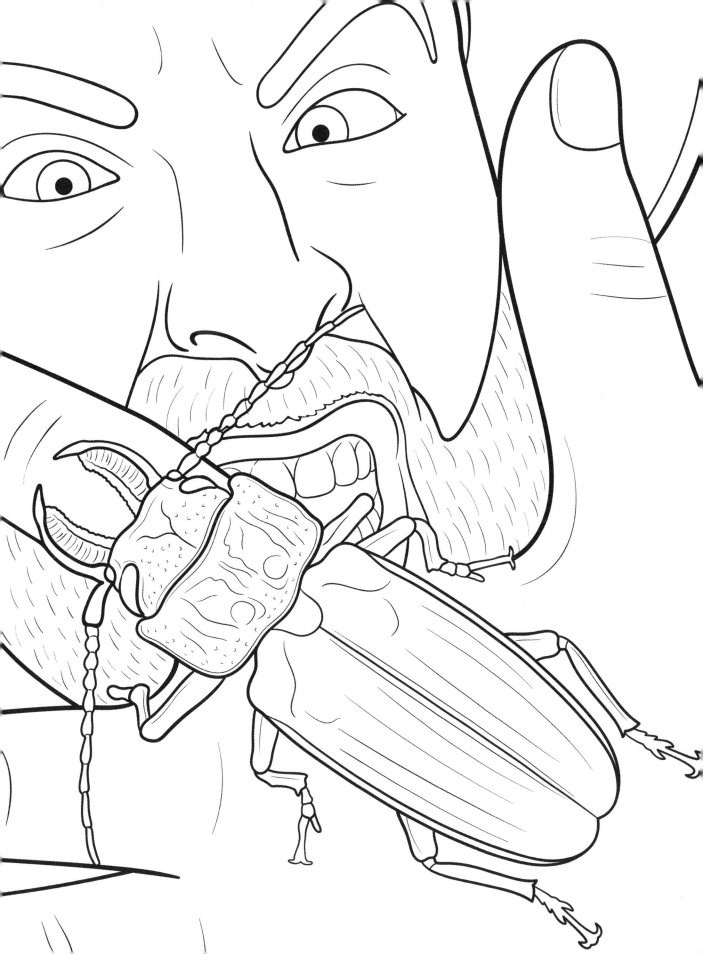

ABOUT THE AUTHORS

Coyote Peterson is an Emmy Award-winning host on YouTube's *Brave Wilderness* channel. With an adventurous nature and a joyful curiosity for wildlife, Coyote's personality creates a friendly and inviting space while getting up close with animals to uncover the true stories behind some of our planet's most misunderstood creatures. Known for his trademark leather cowboy hat, backpack, and bandanna, many fans are driven to emulate him as he educates viewers about the world of animals and fosters a future that conserves environments and their species. Forever dedicated to the joys of storytelling, Coyote is constantly honing his craft to ensure audiences of all ages can partake in his animal adventures.

Mark Vins is an Emmy Award winning wildlife and adventure filmmaker, and the cofounder of the *Brave Wilderness* YouTube channel. Launched in 2014, the channel has become a global sensation growing to nearly twenty million subscribers with over four billion views. Mark began his career behind the camera as a cinematographer, quickly developing his own unique flare for presentation and storytelling. In addition to continuing to produce content for the *Brave Wilderness* channel, he also hosts a variety of programs featuring travel adventures, shark diving, and of course—the wildlife content that made *Brave Wilderness* the sensation it is today.

Mango Publishing, established in 2014, publishes an eclectic list of books by diverse authors—both new and established voices—on topics ranging from business, personal growth, women's empowerment, LGBTQ studies, health, and spirituality to history, popular culture, time management, decluttering, lifestyle, mental wellness, aging, and sustainable living. We were recently named 2019 *and* 2020's #1 fastest-growing independent publisher by *Publishers Weekly*. Our success is driven by our main goal, which is to publish high-quality books that will entertain readers as well as make a positive difference in their lives.

Our readers are our most important resource; we value your input, suggestions, and ideas. We'd love to hear from you—after all, we are publishing books for you!

Please stay in touch with us and follow us at:

Facebook: Mango Publishing
Twitter: @MangoPublishing
Instagram: @MangoPublishing
LinkedIn: Mango Publishing
Pinterest: Mango Publishing
Newsletter: mangopublishinggroup.com/newsletter

Join us on Mango's journey to reinvent publishing, one book at a time.